THE YALE SERIES OF YOUNGER POETS

46

EDITED BY W. H. AUDEN

A BEGINNING

BY

ROBERT HORAN

AMS PRESS

NEW YORK

A Beginning

BY

Robert Horan

With a Foreword by

W. H. Auden

NEW HAVEN

Yale University Press

LONDON · GEOFFREY CUMBERLEGE · OXFORD UNIVERSITY PRESS

1948

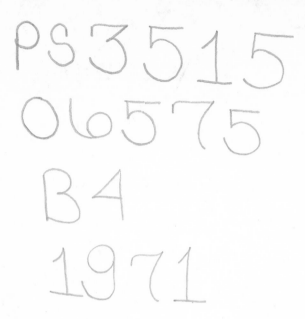
Copyright © 1948, Yale University Press

Reprinted with permission from the edition of 1948, New Haven
First AMS EDITION published 1971
Manufactured in the United States of America

International Standard Book Number:
 Complete Set: 0-404-53800-2
 Volume 46: 0-404-53846-0

Library of Congress Card Catalog Book Number: 75-144752

AMS PRESS, INC.
NEW YORK, N.Y. 10003

For Samuel Barber
and Gian Carlo Menotti

Foreword

To write poetry a man must be endowed with two quite distinct gifts, a love of language and a private vision of the public world. The love of language makes him a versifier and comes, therefore, at least logically, first since, while all verse is not poetry, all poetry is verse and immediately recognizable as such even if it is as "free" as it is in Rimbaud's *Un Saison en Enfer* or St.-J. Perse's *Anabase*.

The diction, for example, of a poet whose love of language is deficient is either too conventional—the noun dictates its own adjective, the rhyme distorts the sense—or too self-consciously strange—when a common adjective or rhyme is really needed he dare not believe it: similarly, his rhythmical patterns are either too mechanically strict or the variations so wildly arbitrary that any sense of an underlying pattern is lost.

Mr. Horan passes both these tests of a good versifier. In "Soft Swimmer, Winter Swan," for example,

> Sped by the building cold and rare in ether, birds hasten
> the heart already taxed with cloud and cherubim—
> fretted heaven, strained songless and flown dim.

he shows that he knows when to use a plain word and when to use a baroque one. In "Litany" the meter varies all the way from

> Among the skeletons of sun
> where the yellow lions run

goes one in a diamond color,
tears on his antique shoulder.

to

Even as I
to his lion's side will fly,
or with feathery fastness
to his feast,

and yet the poem preserves a rhythmical unity.

In the end, of course, it is not the poet's technique but his vision which decides the value of his work. A man either loves language or he doesn't, yet, if he have but a seed of this love in his heart, by reading and hard work, he can make it flower into a true passion. His vision of life, on the other hand, cannot be developed in this way; it is probably given him in the beginning once and for all, and his life task is to explore it further and express it more completely. Here reading and conscious study are little help; indeed they may become a hindrance tempting him away from what he actually sees to what they suggest to him that he ought to see. It is always difficult for any poet to be indifferent to fashion (to be ashamed of being fashionable is as bad as being proud of it) and to remember that, to adapt a remark of Rossini's, all kinds of poetry are good except the boring kind. In some periods it has been the poet with the eccentric vision who found it hardest to dare to be himself; in ours it is more often the other way around—the poet whose gift is, say, for straightforward lyric statement of immediate feeling is frightened into trying to be metaphysical or apocalyptic.

Mr. Horan is fortunate in that not only has he been granted an exciting and unique vision of the world, but also, as is evidenced by "Second Geography," a poem written in

[8]

his teens, discovered early the kind of poetic treatment for which it called.

>   . . . Horses move
> their separate maps, pause in the hands of rocks.
> This is an exile from crystal and sand:
> to walk in the simple wood, through days
> of leather and cobbled rain. To stand
> at gates, outside Arabia, their ears beating,
> hooves in the copper hills of histories.

What excites Mr. Horan here, as in many of his best poems, "The Sun," "The Lesser Kingdom," "Clean, Cool, Early," is the contrast between the natural time in which the creatures live, their "arctic, miniature, unwrinkled world," and the historical time which, for better or, more usually, for worse, man creates by his acts of living.

In Italian painting or in Renaissance poetry like Gongora's *Las Soledades*, nature is a setting for the godly or the civilized life. Hills, waters, woods, birds, and beasts are redeemed and made beautiful and friendly by the Madonna or the Venus whose love has gathered them about her. In Wordsworth nature is more independent but still directly related as the teacher, now comforting, now alarming, now obscure, from whom, if one is only attentive and sensitive enough, one can learn how human life should be lived. In Mr. Horan's poems, on the other hand, as in most poetry of our time, nature is the other-than-man, other even than the child.

> These are sand wastes or wet worlds, foreign and far,
> the least inch of Africa reappearing everywhere,
> in the rock garden, in the lilac bushes.
> They share, like loftier kingdoms,
> zones of danger, sleep and hunger and desire.

[9]

But have they gallows, mock trials, and murder?
Have they pistols, kings, and papers?
Have they cages, chains?

"History," said Stephen Daedalus, "is the nightmare from which I would awake," but this is not possible, indeed it is precisely this attempt to escape being a historical creature that makes man's history a nightmare. To try to live the natural, unhistorical life is to be "fooled in sleep" and perish, while

waking brings back, not where we were,
but where we are.

In a very beautiful poem, "The Little City," Mr. Horan observes the world of the spider.

By evening the web is heavy with monsters,
bright constellation of wasps and bees,
breathless, surrendered.
Bronze skeletons dangle on the wires
and a thin wing flutters.
The medieval city hangs in its stars.

Spider lumbers down the web
and the city stretches with the weight of his walking.
By night we cannot see the flies' faces
and the spider, rocking.

Were the city of man what we should have made it, it would possess the innocence and grace of the spider's city; as it is, the resemblances are accusations. Nature has indeed much to teach us, but chiefly by her refusal to be a support, by the cold shoulder she turns on every motion on our part of idolatry or nostalgia.

W. H. AUDEN

Contents

[11]

Twenty-one Years

CAME with wind and warning this morning
the first birds. Came sun polishing
the crucifix-insect where he paused
dew-instant. I beheld here and there
spiders going in grass to a thread cathedral,
and a round serpent holding both our breaths;
saw, on the twigs, the calligraphy of snails,
and ants marching on the flower-wheels.
Chariots carried all of the living down today.

Who will know later that the light was particular,
betraying by one or many signs a place,
a time arrived at in dandelion summer
that I might stop to look at the underside
of my memories, and slip from each hand
the stitched veil of a year?

Failure follows a ship on a voyage of Sundays,
but leaving a sea-greened cross to catch or drift to.
(Shirts make flags; visitors pass and will rescue.)
Listed in the boat, we turn toward lost, resighted
and prodigal island, mirage of our miracles.
But today will whirl especial in the water, will push
to a pilgrimage. The sight of a continent breaking
over the boat fountains me forward from purgatory.

On the channel the sea returns the faces
of friends in a grey mirror, their names
in the leaves of a book, washed beneath me
on the whitening wave, their flesh flashed
through this wilderness to make my cargo.

[13]

Today, the middle of a morning, I run after
any sight or sorrow, loud to discover sun
in the weather of shadow. Narrower now
by a year, called farther away and fixed faster
to a sail, leaving father and a last look
toward the back-swelling children's horizon.
But dearer than these, I go in a bird's direction
to a holiday country, priest of a water and a world.
Over the blue edge of the map with the flying fish,
that last year may not find my future face,
my hunting or haunted image frozen toward west.

The End of Delight

SOME saffron summer, crossed with a silk sunshine,
leaf-shot in light, lining my black feet
with rims of glitter, brimming the grey grain
and drowning the dry and diamond-headed wheat
in a gather and daze of shoulder-warming heat,

has some such summer come? sealing the blossom,
filling the cradles of water with weighty fish,
swelling the yellowing stars, flushing the fountain
in drops and garlands, fastening the flesh
that blood can no longer leap toward the red mountain?

Hung on the edge of a wave the fruit trembles,
slides like a tear on the window of the air,
falls in a whisper like a breaking bubble;
threads snap; birds blink; the dust on the stair
lifts like a page and settles everywhere.

This sudden summer sprung from all the trees,
from wells, from rocks, riant, rushed, complete,
strikes silent at the peak. I, on my knees,
will strain through surprise to remember, to repeat
the shift, the shock, the death in every street.

I, in my graves, in safe and secret sleep,
wrapped in the dolphined seas, alone in ships
that slide through the wash of days, that sometime slip,
weak in the wood, dissolving all their shapes
in windy worlds and watery mishaps,

will recall the grass kingdom and the scattered dew
strung with the bell and bubble of midnight;
that earlier arc of summer, fabled by few
birds swinging on the grey branch of the light;
the death of a dim star; the end of delight.

Will remember the floating world thundering still,
poised on the brink of breath, shudder and fade;
and the luminous chalk-and-cricket-covered hill
explode, like the parchment heart, burst in its bed
of layered blood and story-dazzled dead.

Beethoven's Heiligenstadt

WHERE is the moment sewn unseparate,
whole sight and sound delivered down
to one listener, looking and looked upon?
He sleeps in his windmill-castle,
sleeps while the wooden arms unwind
their archaic clock in the counting wind.
The listener now lies drowned
in faint and soundless weather
and quiet ground.

Rising, he looks from the wide window
through May-amazing morning, pale meadows
where sheep rise chilled from sleep
and stumble through dewy shadows.
He looks far out and strains to catch
all that was lost:
the sound that once fell forward on the ear
in fresh festivals of fire;
the wheat in a windstorm; wooden wheels
and rivers banked with birds.
A music to shake light and shout out,
all trumpeted together on cool air,
from the thrush to the thunder, clarion clear!

Now this is done in him, sunk like a choir of bells
in miles of water; he lies like some lion lost,
failing even the roar of anger or the peal of praise.
He walks in the hushed streets, in the grey Eden
where children chain, their heels ringing stones.
They stop in the doorway as he passes,

pause as at a funeral procession,
following with white eyes this mild monster
wrapped in the wide cloak, refusing pity.
What ruin does he find in the wavering city;
what memory wreathes him in the rippled rivers,
and wasted song?

The parchment that lies at his hand holds
in pitiful prison all bells, May mornings,
waterfalls and wells; the lion-legion,
the leaves and the lightning.
Here he has rushed down all he could remember,
salted with sorrow, bound in the knots of ink,
pastoral as angels before the silence struck.

Doomed to one house and head, one heaven
and one star's station, did this silence
silence him, deaf but not dead
to the crumbling constellation?
Or did, instead, the crippled crown,
rough in resurrection, sing where swallows
could not follow, and raising its ruined head,
rush all memory back past recollection?

Litany

AMONG the skeletons of sun
where the yellow lions run
goes one in a diamond color,
tears on his antique shoulder.

He walks in a sea of salt
with intention to exalt;
to scatter the green miles
with blessings of exile.

Even as I
to his lion's side will fly,
or with feathery fastness
to his feast,

as birds surround
a glistening wound;
my body endangering
the moment of his angeling.

The most amiable and best belovéd host.
Of these he is my God longest,
and shall be least lost
and last blessed.

Little City

SPIDER, from his flaming sleep,
staggers out into the window frame;
swings out from the red den where he slept
to nest in the gnarled glass.
Fat hero, burnished cannibal
lets down a frail ladder and ties a knot,
sways down to a landing with furry grace.

By noon this corner is a bullet-colored city
and the exhausted architect
sleeps in his pale wheel,
waits without pity for a gold visitor
or coppery captive, his aerial enemies
spinning headlong down the window to the trap.

The street of string shakes now and announces
a surprised angel in the tunnel of thread.
Spider dances down his wiry heaven to taste the moth.
A little battle begins and the prison trembles.
The round spider hunches like a judge.
The wheel glistens.
But this transparent town that caves in at a breath
is paved with perfect steel.
The victim hangs by his feet, and the spider
circles invisible avenues, weaving a grave.

By evening the web is heavy with monsters,
bright constellation of wasps and bees,
breathless, surrendered.
Bronze skeletons dangle on the wires

and a thin wing flutters.
The medieval city hangs in its stars.

Spider lumbers down the web
and the city stretches with the weight of his walking.
By night we cannot see the flies' faces
and the spider, rocking.

Sun

James Agee

lays around us his wealth of arms, a soldier of bloom.
nd armor he raises the roses and worms.
walk unmasked in his love, a broom-colored world,
strangers under his pitiless dominion,
nding his million palms. His bold shower
izzies the beggar, dances the head of the lover.
We rest as the tulip works, and are weak with night,
with the light elastic rain clocking the window;
its blue highways cross our dreams like tears.
But then we arise, sun's subtle song beneath our doors,
his fresh found fire lighting up our lids.
He dots with sparks the milk in the raw kitchen,
flames like a lit spider in the knot of glass;
whereupon we look out, handless, heartless with hope
upon the day. He sings in all our puzzled throats.

Our morning walk is dappled, and the garden swings
through its layers of gloom slowly into light.
The shoes are splashed with shine and the wrist with dew.
A mute celebration is at the foot; iris, violet,
the mouse-bitten bulb and bannered branch
all attest their strength, his grace, my life.
Surely these shafts of emerald, these cups and sticks
pushed from the rustling dark, defeat our prayers.
Their aimless wealth makes poverty of pride;
their splendor a blind effort at surrender,
(as those who love should love, but will withhold;)
cathedrals where no worship is, but light, light!

(Sun, spartar   on the dazed Arab
reeling to hi   meadow of diamond.)

Here in r   ar radiant room,
looking   somewhat see;
draw   , pocket the lavish air
and   gift from letterless latitudes,
sof   upon the mute, straining blossom.
I   flag, fold, buttered and nodding flower,
                  abundance lacing this porcelain harbor.

            c attacking the iris, the wasp patiently
      ing his zones of light, all nature's timid
and battling loves are here alive; they pillage
the knotted grass, swarm the pink air, shine, sing,
stalk in their star-cricket night or lashing noon
all under your marvelous and weighty hand.
Even the spider leans from his cradle of rocks:
you stand like a cracked jewel in his daring eye.

Again, sun, and again, unraveling endless flesh
and breath toward our dim stone. Wheresoever this house
and garden with its mount of birds, its swept, locked
and windowless sorrows, shall turn, your wheel dazzles
with charity; your kind, meaningless, rioting heaven
crowns each shaking fool seeking his shade.

[23]

The Drowned Wife

WITH weed and with sea-barley crowned,
the swinging wife, indifferent, drowned,
floats through the bubbles, ticked with time,
washed in a hurricane of lime,
unanimous in doom.

The rescuers bear with them blood,
the starving bring their painted food,
and met at the bank without a sound,
weak with the hour, scuff the ground,
too late for any good.

Husband, stand on the bridge and wait
for your wife to flow under, swollen white,
her drinking face in the losing dark
warped in the wave, wrapped in the rock,
singing beyond sight.

Sewn in the sea, she has fallen far,
wide of our flowers and our war,
troubled with tongues of light.
The water will burn in her bones all night
and loosen her foolish hair.

O leave the deserted banks at last,
wrapped like a hunchback in the mist,
your treasure is wrinkled away;
your bride lies pale and wild in the sea,
and the keys of the sea are dust.

The Loaves, the Fishes

FLOCK, flock up and through our eyes
the double birds. The sun stripes and troubles
water, but stars will turn back shine again;
in night, the sight of cripple and lack
will be replaced with areas of black.

We divide the single flesh of loaves.
(The loves, the repetitions; ripples
and divisions of waxed light; the chaining
shadows; again, green miles of rain.)
Our hearts forever toss their wells of blood.

The fish, burned dark in the sun,
drawn from the tall marbles of water,
filling the baskets, rich with salt.
There shall be more. Like cups of water
loosened from a sea, frost broken out of glaciers,
lizards cut from dragons. The wound is sealed
with salt. The thin seeds remain. Apples explode.
Harvest.

But wind never will move that stone through noon.
Alone, our feet stained memory too soon
with the walk of leaves.
There may be these, but never again be this.

Though the Eye Be Adamant

THE blind look down in ebony, interior humility;
(the deaf decipher sacraments at lips).
They stiffen when the swaying ground displaces their agility
and flutters the compass in their finger tips.

What muffled melody falls on the misted mirror,
distinguished as water from water or thread from thread;
mysterious as the whippoorwill-ghost, but coming nearer,
shaking the lace ladder of nerves with a foreign tread?

The head waits in its arc of air, the grey breath is suspended
anticipating the riot of revelation;
the face in the posture of grace is tight and attentive
like innocent animals arched in expectation.

The blood, then, fenced in flesh, will leap through its laby-
    rinth,
rush through its crystal reefs and gates to a terminal.
These private signals shout, though the eye be adamant;
the pulse, the taste, the touch surprise the external.

Noise drenches them, dazes them, floods them with a fine fire.
As stripes announce a tiger, so the whispering floor
declares a visitor; these secrets, coiled in the ear,
describe the intruder, the hand at the lock on the door.

(To the deaf, the silence which surrounds disaster,
seeing the dish crumble or the lightning strike,
is peaceful as constant thunder, mute as alabaster.
In the morning, all birds and bells will ring alike.)

[26]

Moored by faint cables to the intricate dome of shadow,
waking far under water in a leafless room,
the blind walk out in the painted park, or stand in the
        meadow,
followed by curious deer in the delicate gloom.

Memory fails to embroider their kingdom with flowers,
their oceans with islands, their dusk with a lilac light.
Somewhere the steeple strikes strange and immaculate hours.
When the deer tremble, when the park closes, it will be night.

January

THE shelled flesh will not hold
nor the locked mind heal
its wind of wounds;

only the stone castle of bone
to signal where the blood has flown,
(as winds feel out the skeleton of hounds).

Here in the laced and leaning land
shines, in a ball of ice, his star-leaved hand,
(his body, the death-eaten island).

Beneath the linens of blood and winter
what steel shocks the shell of the water?
(His shoulders lodged in the young hills of the snow.)

The ants sing in the swollen meadow,
the core of the hill is locked in the marrow.
The printed butterflies blow.

In this violet-veined land,
who, taking his hand in his hand,
calling across the woven fields of summer,

hears the dead echo his find;
the birds turn, and, planted in the wind,
stare at the newcomer?

Agenbite of Inwit

I AM moved here so to surround myself
I shall wall in all dragons and desires;
shall suffer their hunger home within myself,
carry the heavy heart where swing their fires
flushing the face of fright, tearing the tree
that blooms in the road that disappears in me.
Then I shall have them caught in the occasion
engineered by breath; a clear constellation
masked by the horizon of the flesh,
swarming the hive, mangered and leashed.
When staked in me, they wheel like failing stars,
fill the blood with abundance and ache air;
drive me to decipher the intricate mile
of habitation that they have, and will awhile.
They blaze, they thirst. Loaded with the light
they lean in me; drinking, drain me white.
Battered awake, I take the interior traitor
who nailed me, the archangel and ringleader;
he with his Lucifer splendor strung at my feet
foams forward; who walked in my wrinkled streets
or hung in the window of my side as still as sleep,
runs wide now to embrace me, and I strike,
stifle, and strain at him, finding his face of rock
a murdering mirror, the father of my disgrace.
Remorse rang down to ruin all I own,
clotted the heart, rotted the rose with the worm.
Eager for anger, he sits in the skull's quarry
armed with a spade to dig back all I bury;
turns coffins over and shakes forth the shame
I felled without a funeral or a name.

[29]

He kisses close; he wears on his reaching hand
five instruments to search the itching wound;
insatiate, asks for alms; in the confessional, throned
in echoes, he drives me to look down, look deeper down,
driven to see him, see myself in him, the zero-zone.
I press now to catch this Judas on my tongue;
betraying myself, to win his chiming town;
by uttering him, break his birth; facing his face
to clothe his damaging whisper with an inviolate voice.
In his rage I release him, knowing I shall be safe
when the prison he provokes with a flaming touch
shakes down upon this Samson its thundering roof.

Second Geography

THE horses rub their wrists on rope
and leap through a green, wooden prison.
Surround these soft engines with images of salt
and they slowly untangle; on stems and tendons
they run toward you, loose and plural bronze.
They are ordained with slotted blood from
silk countries, their heads moving through
sun-wheels, areas strict with flies.
(Chariots, wires and turbans.) Horses move
their separate maps, pause in the hands of rocks.
This is an exile from crystal and sand:
to walk in the simple wood, through days
of leather and cobbled rain. To stand
at gates, outside Arabia, their ears beating,
hooves in the copper hills of histories.

The Lesser Kingdom

OUTSIDE is an aerial kingdom, a galaxy of amethyst,
and bumblebees in haze, with wings like windows
of cellophane stretched on wires. All hover and pause
in a delirium of noise and emerald eyes.
The frogs that shine in fern shall knock in water;
their throats make round mountains, and they ride
on bubbles, the heart of the voyage transparent.
Freckled and serious, they squat on stones;
they snap at flies and smile.

Has this gold wilderness gates and fences?
Crowns and laws and Lucifers?
Have these leaves poverty and palaces?
Is there dominion here? Exile?
As in larger kingdoms, there are prisoners,
traps and webs, spiders scuttling,
and luminous criminals for food.
Has this danger-infested ground
pride in its habitation? ease or agony
or something like despair?
The moths are lost in the strawberries, yes,
or gnats in the blue towers of iris;
there are caterpillars hung on thorns.
But do they feel dark secure, or terror unalterable?
Do they surmise sunset and the fading light
as relief or as an omen?

The threads of antennae explore clover provinces,
but these see outside only;
their hearts are of fur.

The wasp, like the lion,
sleeps with all daggers ready, and lightly on a leaf,
restless at the dim sound of an enemy.
Are they signaled from safety and betrayed,
swallowed by swaying snakes on a warm rock,
poisoned, deceived, dismantled?

Hidden in the blossoming banks on satin haunches,
the panther lifts a paw.
The frogs blink their eyes over the rim of the water,
the pheasants glitter.
At the moment of battle, cockatoos scream;
the branches cloud with pink birds.
Death, there, brings back relaxation
like the loose, wild rain following days of thunder.
The beetles in blue armor and the red ant armies
devour, spear, or sting the unfamiliar.
Many are ruffled in fright or frozen in anticipation.

These are sand wastes or wet worlds, foreign and far,
the least inch of Africa reappearing everywhere,
in the rock garden, in the lilac bushes.
They share, like loftier kingdoms,
zones of danger, sleep and hunger and desire.

But have they gallows, mock trials, and murder?
Have they pistols, kings, and papers?
Have they cages, chains?

Breakage

THE sea recovers its lostness,
breaks its bright windows of light,
but will fill again; stack shelves on shells,
the sound of shudder, the shadow, the shine.

What breaks with the hands does not contain surprise.
The eyes do not stare back, but expect the cone
of honey to split its gold shutter,
be mute, be summer frozen small.

I say all bubbles dissolve; birds become sound
and listen on the rim of barrels for the note
starring the rain water.

But the bells are hard. They bring a black
brilliance over any wall. Their rings spread
and stop coppered bees on the edge of blossom,
run dark through the thickness of trees.

From the shake around a steeple,
I would say bells do not shine, but break.

Palms and Calendars

FOLDED, my tents and stars,
to the double of day returning;
confirmed in the light of wars
and the witness of burning.
Christened and wrapped in straw,
his tiger of scripture
is ribboned with love of law.
No angel will endanger
his wings of sulphur, but unlock
and deliver the breath up to the rock.

So cage the striped and lidded birds, so chain
entrance and April to a wall of rain.
The year's palms and calendars
ring in the heels of the bells.

Such eyes and endeavors
will fail, like apples in their wells
of green and bark; hold them to glass,
whose bones are dark as water was.
Nothing but cloths of clouds will ever trap
this salt and silken martyr in our rooms.
With hands as dry as keys, we guide the map
and the river, floating toward towns of tombs.

On the Pink and Pigeoned Beach

ON the pink and pigeoned beach
fails the amaranthine sea.
The balconies of memory
are washed away like lace.

Underneath the water's stations,
hung like toys in fluid worlds
sea horses gallop through the pearls,
starfish climb their crooked nations.

From the margin where we stand
all our anger is undone;
courts of water ravel on,
parks of emerald paved with wind;

carillon of bubbles holding
fists of weed; and water spiders
crawling up their tinsel ladders
spin the brilliant scaffolding.

Now the limitless and loud
Atlantic falters at our heels,
gathers its surrendered miles
like magnets drawing back the dead;

folds its prodigals again,
noon over noon; lost like needles,
pulled back to their shining stables
bearing torn fruit and flowers in.

Here all our dangers seem a sum
less than love and less than these.
From their marble farms the fish
gambol on to greener homes.

Prometheus

HE pales at pleasure,
dives in his drenched rack
toward the dark;
lies in his ropes and weeps
but wrenched past care
for the hummingbird in passage
through blue air,
past joy in the sparrowed air.
Suns and the planet pearls
sit silent near him, poise
white in their vacant worlds
and strike his chains.
Weak on his rock he smiles
at their fresh fires, free lights
that flesh the morning miles;
feels his body sealed,
the coffin open and the rubbed bone
assailable. A tempest of blood
blinds the rash prisoner in stone,
wet in his midnight flood.

He prays some wilderness of water
to wash over these;
some sea and undulant savior
restore these agonies

out of the random flesh
into the spirit; make Spartan
this small splendor, and wash
clear the clotted curtain.

The church of chains has breath,
breathes with his breath,
moves at his neck and wrist
delaying death.
He feels for the key, wreathed
as he is in slow lead,
bruised by serpents, clothed
in a blaze, diseased.
His hands knock against final bone;
and the molten bird, bright on his billowing stone,
picks at the locks, now strikes
where the heart storms most,
drives with the dagger beak through the lost
islands of his face.

Prometheus, granted this grace,
mistakes devil for deliverer, who sings
brilliant in his embrace,
unknotting the metal strings.
He will not see, when once he is released,
the dark blood shine in the eye of the beast.

Clean, Cool, Early

CLEAN, cool, early,
the stones arched high and hard;
cool, calm, awake
in a light of limes.
Before the leaves melt
and the fine flow alters
the wine-flushed window,
we're held apart in dawn,
rinsed clear.
The stars are rigged for morning,
spare and even,
like the color of water hardened.
Firm, unspotted, and washed
free of its random flesh,
part-frozen, an apple of air.

As with the iceberg-center,
detail is ornament in this weather;
fixed in the flowering ice,
bird, stick, star in ether,
all taste of emptiness, salted
and bottled in cobalt together.

To be late is to miss it,
while the enemy of clarity
makes rapid revision,
reels all in an abundance of light
and drops of false radiance.
It is that light withheld,
moved forward inches in a wind,

interior, that shapes a morning.
Like porcelain or casual sculpture
in ice, this is scorched
by indiscriminate sun,
unlaced in noon.

Seven is an exact moment,
the transit from station to station
when energy has been pulled pale,
but stretched, does not waver,
but full, does not tilt nor falter.
It awakens the smallest animals first.

See yourself here the imperfect stranger
early risen and boated out in blue
mirror upon mirror back to the beginning;
an unfamiliar bird and tall intruder.
Before the leaf loosens,
and between two forms of light,
take time to raise from the frosted dust
and silk-scattered hedges,
the frame of a rose, the ashes of a room,
a fern, a small fire in dew, a paused spider.
These, though moribund in stronger light and years,
may steady memory, serve to identify
an arctic, miniature, unwrinkled world.

O! Mother of My Tears!
Believe for Me! Fold Thy Son!

Finnegans Wake

OUR midnight palaces are mocked by morning;
sold in the sun, the gold-fretted scaffolding
knocked boldly down when the real weather's in.
We all will fall at just a human touch
who weep in dreams or hide inside the stone
that melts like a house of honey on a branch.
Believe for me! Fold thy son!

> I lean in the leaves and listen.
> The drunk bird brightens, rings at my ear,
> Icarion-feathered messenger in air,
> a handful-heaven and careless chanticleer,
> a cadence in a wilderness, a sudden station
> of looped singing, loosed while I crouch here
> wasted in fear, O! Mother of my tears!

And have no hands to serve and none to save.
No heart to haul heavy up, letting the scarlet go
its free way, staining the starched waves,
flooding the statues I have worshiped so;
no heart to knock everywhere and hurl blood
hard against every door, then fall where I stood,
leaving me wrecked in red but lost in love!

> No, but not here, where priests and prisoners crawl,
> locked in the arms of angels on the wall.
> They whisper in their watery chains and cough.

Galled in their ropes, not fallen far enough,
they step where the thorns are thickest, and are blown
back in the wind; they leave a blazing town
to find the fields in flames, and roads of bone.

Believe for me! Some mornings I will waken
to see where the sun has been, and count his hours.
Some days are worked with a wonder unforsaken,
our chainless bodies scattered in the flowers,
free for a moment from the gauze of tears,
swung on like swallows, all our pity done:
O! Mother of my fears! Behold thy son!

A Love Poem

IN the white mansion of my hand
lie engraved my guest;
asleep in the tamed, bony island
hear the heartbeat beast.

Hear the far tides fold and battle,
child, caretaker, O counterpart!
Your drunk king in his park startles
the loud apple of the heart.

Rise in me, singer, when I wake
to see the sun's rude runners
salute, and his bold trumpets mock
all our timid banners.

Be in me the free prisoner, caught
but not cruel, but not captured;
(as the light lips learn untaught
how the face is featured).

Alert in the azure of the eyes,
catch the stumbling blindman.
Be, in the fumbled ship, a breeze
and an aerial engine.

If, in a moon, I slip outside
to mark the turned world,
sing in my shuttered side
and light the low peril.

[44]

Within, you can swim and sweeten
(like springs in the April bark
their cherry-flavored house), and fatten
on the blushed food of the dark.

And I shall surrender summertimes;
quilt with clover the mute desert;
send you those intermittent wines
that flood the fooled heart.

Rejoice in me, then, singer,
sing in the flowered mountain!
Bless, in his night, the fond beginner
at his simple fountain.

Suppose We Kill a King

SUPPOSE we kill a king, and then a king, and then a king;
princes are waiting everywhere;
suppose by poison or by water, kill a queen;
her daughter sits upon the stair.

The beast begun comes back.
Like shadows or like mirrors where they stand,
the sun assassinates, the moon refurnishes
the shadow with a hand.
Lying alone in midnight, drowned in guilt
and staggered with emeralds while they sleep:
the daggers in the bed of silk,
the devils in disguise,
the footman with the hand that shakes,
and when they wake,
the Dauphin with his eyes.

The king will walk, an antlered ghost, through castle halls,
and dukes will turn their heads to see;
the queen will wake to find her face on palace walls
looking down from a tapestry.

A prince, in lighting a taper for a tomb
and putting a sleepy king to bed,
will leave a glistening rapier in his room:
will separate his heart and head
and kneeling at his bleeding crown
and covering the fallen head
will stifle the echo with his gown.

Sidewise in Venetian glass
the mirror shows the murderer, a king.
The bells that rang a funeral
must pause to ring a christening.
The one who killed the king is killed,
assassin, silenced with a stone;
a prison hung around his throat,
a weight upon his tongue.

Like mice beneath a rotting throne, the whispering men
sit in the palace sun,
and as the coffin passes through the towns,
lay down their daggers to put on their crowns.

Sonnets

ANNOUNCED to me by trumpets and by tears,
by tempests in the silk, by paper wars,
how calendars of death in distant years
will well up in our eyes and wall our stars.
In ferns and forests, as the ghost appears
wrapped in his flags or swinging from his shores,
muffled with cautious cloth, we stop our ears,
sing in our sleep to silence all his sores.

Pinned to our wrists like butterflies to glass,
the alphabets of age, the wheels of grief.
A grain of salt, a nail, a lip, a leaf
reminds us that they melt and move through grass.

Announced to me by all they left to keep
how soon they shall assassinate my sleep.

II

Sewn to my side, the shaken ships of love
move in their milky waste of pearls and blood;
let down their thorny nets to fire and flood,
splinter the roof of water, drown the dove.
First, in the breath of morning, all put out
in siren-light and glittering of grace,
savored by weather; at the white lookout
sight simple islands moored in flowered space.

Then, on my banks of flesh, as on a rock,
heave hills and heavens signaling the wreck;
wild on the wave, they thunder in and shock
the red, remote cathedral where I work.

The birdlike boats, bringing their beaks toward home,
spin in my side, sail down and rest on bone.

III

"Such joy comes knocking at the gate of tears,"
wears triumph while he weeps and climbs the stairs;
looks for his kingdom, opens all the doors
on rooms of ashes, ceilings, windows, floors;
looks for the chiming clock and finds it gone;
the grey walls failing, and the rugs like flesh
woven with faded wreaths of frozen sun.
The halls are full of animals and fish.

The children lie asleep wrapped in their blood;
the neighbors walk along a toppling roof;
the gardener digs a grave with arms of wood;
the dogs stare and the birds fall from the cliff.

Such joy, come knocking at the gate of fears,
finds the house fallen in his childhood fires.

IV

In battle with bold angels in the dark,
Michael and the Lucifers we love
must lose. It is an error of the Ark
that animals be paired, eagle to dove.
Balance is death. With man it is intended
angels succumb to our humanity.
Though battle and dark blood be never ended,
the son should win once over vanity.

The fatal folly of our parents is
a victory of years. This wisdom tears
the child in his tower, the child in his
intricate terror, innocent of wars.
Angels must fall before the fall of man;
the father loses first, and then the son.

V

Returned to my town of trees, the summers start
their love in leaf, and flower in the walls;
into the medaled morning, April falls
as far as the acre from heart to heart.
In white aisles of my chest and chaliced bones
another flower starts in deeper farms.
Christened with light and capped with hidden thorns
I sleep in the crypt and cradle of your arms.

Now boated back, wept on my river home,
I see the wasp-and-violet-scattered mountain,
once a dark pasture of obsidian
when last I left it wrapped in rain and storm,
ablaze in its armor of bonfire-fountains
and final, miracle meridian.

VI

Some mornings in cold masonry expose
their bloom in huts of ice, fed with a fire
that shatters what it shows, shows us a rose
mounted immaculate in ample air.
Coined quietly in calm, then hurried forth
under the wheeling stars, was resurrected.
Muffling its green machinery, this earth
molded and seamed, cold rose on rose erected.

And underground, the weather that has hollowed
stone from around the heart, is still dissolving
those grey and fallen sculptures, to be followed
thorn upon thorn and red on red revolving
in faultless succession as the bowered ocean,
unveiling the architecture of devotion.

VII

The dark feeds us the dark, the leaden word;
hangs up its leafless heaven when we've looked,
and halting when the knock of light is heard,
we close the eyes, let the bold dead lie locked.
The heart sings in its stone, but when we've knocked
falls still, held like the frightened singing bird
hearing the hunter; stops when he has heard,
hung on the branch of terror, mute and mocked.

As prisoners, faltering at the shock
of light from an opened door, will step back,
back through their hunger to familiar dark,
lean on the bars and let the bars lean back,
we're fooled in the fabled dark, afraid to see
the cage will crumble if we lift the key.

VIII

Corn-colored children of our paradise
hang naked in the trees, ageless in ice,

summerless shadows caged in cold surprise,
their crowns of faded feathers dark with lice.
Or fixed in featureless dust where they fell,
their bleeding mothers staring from their eyes,
they sleep like frozen dwarfs. Our victories
halo their heads; our pity wreathes them well.

The starving pose for photographs. Their cries,
like crazy toys, molest the infidel
angry at agony. These fleshless dice
brighten the fields, empty of asphodel.
Their voiceless terror tells us like a bell
our heavens are inhabited with hell.

IX

Another summer sealed and still no sign
except, in the doomed grass, the frantic beetle
struggling against a moving pole of wind
toward his brown sleep in the leafy steeple.
Another sun outshone and still no word
except the mute box hanging in the wood
where warblers and the Persian hummingbird
performed their aerials undisturbed.

Another winter waits and still no strength
to live in love and walk against our tears;
but only time moves on its stars at length,
and on and on through years and years and years.

Another dreamer wakes and still no proof
he lies awake and under his own roof.

X

When love is pity then it is perverse;
fed on a stolen fruit, will nourish none,
but, like lost sailors, swing from worse to worse,
whose waves no waters are, whose star's undone.
This coronation of a crippled king
will blacken statues and turn wax the flower;
he cannot kiss whose mouth's devouring
dust for bread and centuries for an hour.

This charity is cool that fools the arms
and sets false fires in the dwindled night.
When love is pity, all the blood's alarms
should ring the sleeper from his dead delight.
Then, in red morning, he may see them move,
love and pity down each separate grove.

Song for Jane Bowles

OUR world's lost half its light;
it's dimming down
steady now and dumb
like a weathered town
in English midnight.

As the gold rust goes
from the garden rose,
through the lashes of the eye
see a leaner sky
bereft of blues.

Childhood's capped clowns
jingle no more.
What we later wear
we can't remember.
The fool in the face frowns.

The room gets smaller,
the door tight and low;
and the brushed snow
is at the window.
March is a jailer.

We fix the dark fires
and climb the stairs,
and no one hears
the loose light tears
and no one cares.

Soft Swimmer, Winter Swan

THE sun shows thin through hail, wallpaper-pale, and
    falls
grey from its royal world toward colder poles.
Gone, like a grave swan gone blossoming in bone,
a white tree of feathers, blown singly down.

A last, a light, and caught in the air-ladder lark,
south-driven, climbing the indian, swift dark, and listen!
Sped by the building cold and rare in ether, birds hasten
the heart already taxed with cloud and cherubim—
fretted heaven, strained songless and flown dim.
Out from the house that held them in safe summer,
small ponds and blue counties, the chequered swimmers
in air, spring sudden through the closing vault of frost.
(The last, awakened by a late storm, are forever lost.)

But the calm swan, adamant in autumn, passes
through still willowed water, parting the yellow rushes.
His eye, like a lighted nail, sees the vast
distance of amethyst roll under him, the marble beast.

Seen from the shore, this bird but luminous boat,
so motionless in speed, quiet, will float
forward in cold time, disdaining harbor; marooned
in infinite roads of rivers, his wings wrought around
to muffle danger and battle with the wind;
safe, slow, calm, a ship with frail lights, a white swan.

But seen from beneath, the soft statue hardens; the wild feet
must wrest from this pure prison some retreat,

outdistance winter and oblivion; now, in feverish motion, foam
the careless waters, throat, wing, heart, all spotless in arched
    bone.

Pressed, must push farther on through lakes where winter
    lies
secret and dumb in shallows, building bright fields of ice
to trap the transparent fish, turn the wet world to stone,
surprise the soft swimmer and capture the winter swan.

We see, serene, this desperate passage through perfect seas;
taught to see ease in agony, see only ease.
In the battle of snow against snow and wind upon wind
the dead lie fooled in the ice, too far to find.

Song

WHO carries coin and crown
comes from the seaside down,
destroyer of my town.

And in the halls of wheat
you hear his serpent feet
like feathers in the heat.

Along my vein and bone
his arrowhead of stone
drives the lost blood toward home.

Who makes my heart his room
is silent when I come
as moss within a tomb.

His head of love, his hands of lace
unwind my final hiding place.

In the Snow-world

THE word leaves our lips in ice;
warped in a glass, is meaning visible,
speech become frost, and love with weight.
Where we step, the inches of the world
sink in a little, filling up the wound.
All are in their houses, looking out.
The birds, wrapped in a room of string,
blink back at the light, remembering
yesterday's noisy rain and hammering
today turned solid, like a burial.
In scarlet holes in hills the foxes
find the air too tight to breathe,
stretched thin and shared by many miles.
They turn now in their sleep of leaves,
and hearing death break faintly in a bugle,
run low like a ribbon, escaping, through the trees,
the teeth of the horse, the hunter like an eagle.
Somewhere the deer are leaping in the weather
surprised by the gentle ways and shapes of water.
With no leaf left, the snow brings bread,
a showered communion over all the trees;
foils and fills the branches, pillowing
the rock they lean in, crowning limbs
with a cold halo of ice and a glistening.
And all are afraid of the absence of sound,
as of something missing. Tunneling underground,
the mole stops at a frozen, black horizon;
the bat, hung like leather from his feet,
swings silently, his eyes closed twice
against this mystery. And with humanity,

[63]

the road that leads into the village
shows monuments, implies a cemetery.
The children's snowmen with luminous black eyes
will wistfully melt, a broom their wooden weapon
against the flashing minute of winter sun.
Over their porous cheeks, like ink in cotton,
flow charcoal tears. We stand in the center
to see the world fall down from its arch,
caught, as our own far heaven disappears
and everyone else's heaven is getting closer,
covering us with memories and years.
Like the man, the size of a thimble, stuck
in the solid and circular glass of childhood,
with neither a sun nor a moon; when it is shook,
the whispering wild world of snow and light
smothers him under for our own delight.

Gabriel

Down all the marble miles
and doorways of despair
find perpetual exile
expectant there.

This is my Gabriel
whose spectacular, aerial
agility is angel's wax
to melt upon my rocks.

It is breath to this ghost
in his heart's hills lost;
and it is miracle's nail
hammered to my heel.

Expectant, as if to watch;
silent, to catch;
like a clarion of history
announcing an agony.

His birds sing lonely
in a wooden town.
His paper ceremony
trumpets me home.

Jumping Midnight Salmon

THIS is a scene of my imagination:
guided by wet lamps toward the choiring water,
the silver wharf wood splinters at our heels
and crooked ropes trip the drunk stargazer.

Those leaning, fragile, melancholy houses
seen at the seaside loom here also,
although this journey takes us to a river.
I can hear the thin wives in their iron beds.

I know the damp children are dropped in sleep,
and the sailor folded in his farm of green.
On the porch, the red-eyed dreaming dog
smells the lantern moving like a moon.

After some hours inland, our hearts bright with beats
in the bold midnight that dews the jacket,
we come to a little shelf hung over the river,
and our blond lamps dazzle the swinging fog.

Like Indians, first one and then another
crouches on haunches close to the coiling water;
leans his drawn face down toward the rapid mirror,
the muscular unfolding meadows.

And there, below, twined in a million armors,
they weave and shine, arched in the pebbled dark;
loop their escape through all this world's windows
in cold joy, the jumping midnight salmon!

Hurricane Lamp

THE hushed bell of the lamp
guards a grey light
against the damp,
as an immutable skeleton
cages the heart.
It suffers us to sight
flaws in the fiery dark,
to save one dwindling sun
against all shock.
It gives wilderness a glow
of ready vermilion,
poised to overthrow
whatever leaning lion
is wrestling in the snow.
This light, like the slipping moon,
surrenders slow.

Now, in a wrecking wind,
we feast our fears
at this cold shrine;
find harbor in pale wealth
and white fires.
I see myself
printed within the glass
and blind with a tear.
Banked between wars
this small safety shines.

The spiral hurricane
rushes the stairs to the heart;

drenched with mercurial rain
the wires spark,
the chandelier has dropped
through the wet roof of the dark.
We lift a match to watch
the luminous leaves go down
over the raging meadow
and the crooked town.

Inside the iron frame
the fastened flame
widens like a whisper taking sound
and illuminates our ground.
We open doors; we listen
and hear all seasons pass
while the gold thread in the glass
climbs and glistens.

This knife of light releases
our trapped breath.
After the storm is over,
it shows us on the lawn, beneath
the weight of death,
tomorrow's clover.

Fooled in Sleep

ON waking, feel the lion light
loom over you; the gaunt and graceless room,
faced squarely, wheel back bright;
the curtain part over the rocking heart.
Lifting the head up from its warm cave,
will tears swarm sudden over a lonely arm?
As rain wrecks silence or sparkles dark,
so morning may be marred by memory,
marked by remembrance as an enemy.
Fooled in sleep, are you now surprised
at this pitiable, pale paradise?
The day world wading toward you, pier by pier?
Where once you washed so steep in sleep
hung with a dumb weight, frozen and caught,
there tragedy was secure and terror pure;
the beasts at last roamed back into their towns
and the remote miles of bone.
Within that ravening sleep you heralded danger
at least with a splitting cry; dodged death
in instant recognition; gathered breath.
So hope is restored at morning
with a solider despair.
You suffer pity when you wake,
widening the stone gaze to include
a signal solitude, a chalk and marble maze.
Each ghost floats forward with a famished face.
Discover yourself so deeply occupied,
so weaponless, it empties terror even,
exposing a faded heaven.
As the branched sleep is broken,

the tears harden, and the tongue
is tired, not yet having spoken.
As the heart shrinks and the five fingers
relax their star,
waking brings back, not where we were,
but where we are.

Antiphonal Song

WHAT is it eats the hunter's breath
    as he picks through the thicket?
The blood that's bound to bleed to death
    like a leak in a bucket.

What is it tires the oarsman so
    as he climbs the chaste water?
The love that he leaves and the winds that blow
    him on green miles after.

What is it drains the drinker there
    at the jumping fountain?
The desert he crossed that brought him there
    and the next mountain.

The Lark-hunter

KISSES her cold sleeping mouth in the dark.
Promising victory, straps on his belt of bullets,
his knives and nets, the boots, the jacket,
all of the apparatus of fear,
and leaves her dreaming.
He studies the light muffled in the curtains
as he drinks his coffee.
He washes his hands.
His heart building, walks out through
the full meadow toward the trees.

All objects come awake like angels
around him. In a desert of fog and dawn
a delicate world assembles.
He lays nets for the thronging larks,
plants his poisons, prepares the grave throne.

Wet-winged still and dazed in dew
they shake forth slightly, singly,
then in high crowds in an aerial uproar,
a beginning of banners, a contagious flutter
like the catching of small flames.
Now their innocence is their danger.

These larks in the surprise of sunrise
start adoration. The flight of the heart
in the throat, the light, the note,
explain to us generous grace,
the futility of envy. In madrigal chorus
they offer us their constant crowns.

They sing in the flawless grottoes of ether.
Driving the night's last nightingales apart,
propose antique elegies; sing surrender
to being and beaded morning.

The hushed hunter watches in the bush;
dismisses the bold bluejays,
charmed in the midst of danger
like lucky horses in a carnival.
They fly on free to join the vesper sparrows,
safe as the bells, inedible angelus
whose tongues are too rough velvet for his taste.

Dismisses, too, the goldfinches,
rocketing birds with bad flesh;
all safe in their domes,
lights that will not be eaten tonight,
may riot in rich weather.

Reprieved also, martins and cardinals,
various day birds, wrens and orioles,
the hermit thrush among his violets,
too thin or wild or common for his touch.
These may be wary only of thunder,
snakes, lice, stones, and boys.

But the first-found lark is marked,
caught for a Lorelei, trained to betray.
The hunter blinds the lark.
Tied to a tree with a string, to sing
undistracted in midnight that was morning,
he hunts for the hunter like a magic toy.
Dim in delirium, the charmed captive sings.

All the larks listen from far boughs
to the sudden flood, the blind solo.
From memorized leaves they are summoned down.
Disarmed by love from their gold games,
they surround like curious, listening seraphim;
join him in the fire, and the trap springs.

Now they fumble in the net, lit by terror,
caught in a clock like silk; their agate eyes,
their agonies, a proof, a gift, a bracelet to the victor.

If it has been a good morning,
the sun solid and early to dazzle,
the hunter may carry home tumbled dozens
of singers in his leather coffin.
And, sometimes among them, an accident
of abundance, a savorless intruder
like the pale prince of a distant county,
foreign as a lion at a feast of ants,
a bitter swallow or nameless feather.

The hunter is chilled from waiting,
posturing in shadow like a statue,
patient until the wild mistakes of love
crowd his bright net.
Tall, tense, armed against the air,
now his heart beats softer in its sea.
The proud assassin limps home with his prize,
swings home with his supper to his kisses,
a branch of cold larks on his stained shoulder,
a wife waiting to wash out the murder.

The Queen's Face on the Summery Coin

THE queen's face on the summery coin
was never golder nor more regal
than his body's bright and bursting bugle
where once it walked between the stripes of rain.

The birds swing in their appled cages
and the solid sun will walk
through straw houses where honey rages
churning the light to chalk.

The wind shines on the woody grove.
We live in a copper clock where, on the hour,
a polished bell divides the stem and flower
and drains the ghost-built body of its love.

Like the deaf listening for a silence
that follows no sound,
or the sick swung in the balance
between wound and wound,

there is too much eye to see
all but the nearest disorder.
In the sable shadow of this harbor
he lies him down among the singing bees.

On Martha Graham's *Deaths and Entrances*

BECAUSE I have no death to breathe backward into,
so little life to lie lovingly on,
less and less savior to kneel and balance to,
none to bless, none to crucify, no, not one;

though I have left all gates and windows open
to rain and strangers in the fire-faced storms,
only the lost, the mad, the murdered enter
weak with weeping and crowned with indelible thorns.

How narrow the figures, moved on a chequered mile;
hooded bishops and kings with painted eyes
who mock at the mirror of rage, stand speechless while
the body betrays its old agonies.

Because the desperate mind demands witness,
and all the guilty seek conspirator,
I must confess, with none to strike or kiss,
myself the invisible tormentor.

Mariner

THIS fever shall melt rocks,
shall rot the heart;
this fire leap in the clocks,
wring them to wax.
Shall sting at the start,
stifle and depart.

This fever will unfasten
the sun from the word;
drain peace, and fashion
pride in the place of passion;
crumble the loud bird.
Sing, swallow, sing unheard.

This fever films the eyes;
in its seas, drowns twice
the word-wild mariner
pinned to his ship of ice.
The sea-staggered stranger
is blistered with danger.

Temptation, safe at first,
will riot under thirst;
his face in the clear cobalt
shine back without a fault,
surrendering to the worst,
feast on the fatal salt.

Now thin with terror, float
over the rocking rim.

Gulls in the azure swim,
fall on the bones in the boat,
the bubble of blood in the throat.

Do not go after him.

A Beginning

I

FROM the lusterless prison where we pray,
the inside house veiled in vermilion,
look out to the morning-shaken season,
the window, the winter, the abundant day.

Follow these arrows through a wilderness
while the birds and suns are dropping down,
and the papery world dissolves its illness;
all trumpets are playing in all towns.

One, through the green glass of his eye,
sees in his voyage chariots and ashes
wrapped in the multiple flesh of mystery;
the ransom of his sleep, and fabled faces.

Sees the doom in the dark, the instant unraveling,
the sun roping the berries and the branches;
sees the clock stop and the panther springing,
the serpent on the gilt and glittering fences;

the morning-beaded tree, the widening spring,
filled like a bubble balanced on a rock.
This is his topless tower. The room is glistening,
is starred and teared and trembles at a look.

Now, in his morning-house, his bed, his jail,
his room, the wave, wherever he is lying,
he looks far out and fails, he falls and fails.
And, inward, looks on calmly at the dying.

So the creator in the middle of creation
is desperate, like a witness to the elated
luminous angel exploring a secret nation.
He is amazed and dazzled, he is created.

II

(The triumph of the prison and the priest
is terror and contrition, is the feast
of father and son devouring one host
by the rich hands of God severely blessed.)

Struck on the wrist by an ancestral satan,
he sees himself the son of this sad sultan.
He lifts his face to the glass wherein each feature
doubles his guilt against his ghostly Father.

Trapped by this phantom in a faded room,
half a cathedral, half the walls of home,
he hears the last clock striking in the hall,
he hears his shadow falling and he sees his fall.

Those who came before him follow after,
stuck in his side, the hungry weeping clowns,
the deathless families, the breathless daughters,
each ancestor armed only with a stone.

And chariots roll over him like clouds.
Into the face of fired and flying weather
he rushes with the winds around him loud.
He is no longer yours, nor you his Father.

From the white hilltop, from the heavy heaven
hanging about your shoulders like a sword,

[80]

out from your shaking house he will be driven
without a wish, a warning, or a word.

If, in the purple act, the lion-warrior
drops, doubled on his dagger to the hilt,
his doom his own, shadowed with no savior,
forgotten in black gardens of his guilt,

if, in the wraith of dust, he falls too far,
you may condemn him from a humming star.

III

I am that he,
that him controlled by fathers
and whose fate
is finished in those fiery waters.

I am that one
so longing for excess,
from the unborn
comes forward to amaze.

I am that one
whose least and lightest breath,
shrunk to my solitude,
is patched and plumed with death.

He is to me
drawn tight as the root of a s   low,
by the marginal sea
or the mild milkweeded meadow.

[81]

I am that one
deceived in charmed and radiant rain;
again, in charioted sun,
am the son enchained.

I am that one
nailed lonely to the loud landscape
he knew at first;
inward only, and without escape.

IV

Before the sun's begun, it's gone!
The birds, the apples in that dawn
lie red, fly bannered in that blood,
a hushed, illuminated flood.

Where waters run, bend down,
dive deep and draw to harbor the unknown.
At the first, clockless minute in the east
be warm and walking in it once at least
before the counterfeiting sun has crossed
the melting angel hidden in the beast.
Be singular and early here. Be mercy's host.

By noon the trees are dumb, the plume of thunder
plunges in the wood and through the water;
the salmon strike at the dark turned under,
the metal, million, anonymous welter.

See, through the sand, a star where mornings are,
through the hand, a rose dissolve.

Ashes are quieted by a tear,
and the winds in the worlds revolve.

Is it within one day, by the trick of a cloud,
that the shadow of sun is turned toward us,
the double disaster revealed, and the cured
fallen back on his dark bed, breathless?

So death delivers none but marks many.
Stigmata, token, coin of conscience
consume us at the pinnacle; money
falls from our hanging hands like penitence.

We kneel where we sometime stood; we pray
against all of the glittering devils, or lie alone
in loss of love, dazzled by ghosts of a day,
the mutiny of a minute turned and gone.

Bewildered by a bloodless death
or agonized by lack of breath
and frightened by the portent of a wreath,
we burst the cage of glass to find the bride,
destroy the tree to see the bird inside.

Let sorrow a little earlier deliver
each from his own security and fever,
from his belief in angels without sin.
When we are done with glory we begin.

V

I am that one who grieves
in winter the wide wind,

the architect of water and of leaves,
the sculptor of a house of cloud or bone,
investigator, shaping the sharp stone.

Today the trees are flown in frozen rooms,
wired to the floors of snow.
Washed clear of ornament, they show
winter's spare statuary without a spark.
We walk here on the ridges of the heart;
on stones wrapped in the ice wrapped in the park
wrapped in the wet rectangle of the dark.

The center of the ice is green, pretending spring.
By listening at the fissure in the pond
I can hear the rippled breath expiring,
and recognize the end.

Marooned inside the winter lake,
inside the carbon castles of the fish,
arrested by the frozen weight,
I lie in the solid world that earlier flowed,
flowed onward toward a disappearing home,
without a sea to fly to, but in a circle moving,
with stations of green rest and moving slow.

I, like the fish, who found their last delight
stopped in this congealing of the light,
this burial in a star.
Awake and pink and petrified
they sit in the salt and stare
while the white horizon falters
and the direction is anywhere.

VI

Captured in these northern mountains
flawed with the greening sticks of spring,
I hear in the ice far, fiery fountains,
the free, muted fountains beginning.

Then stairs and hills of ice dissolve,
prisons fall open at a whisper,
the winds in the turned worlds revolve,
the grey jails of the fish surrender.

I ride with them down the rough shallows,
endlessly on as streaming swallows
entering, unerring, everywhere
the new, blue levels of the air.

My father's statues lie in pools of wax;
the dark devoured, the rocks unlocked.
The bird, the unbridled horse, plunge in the light.
The wells break open and the world is fountaining,
with slivering sound and nightingale-noise night,
a breathless start, a heart, and a beginning.